In Celebration of

. . . .

Date

. . . .

Welcome little one!

Baby details

Name _____

Born _____

Time _____

Weight _____

Height _____

Thoughts & Messages

_____

_____

_____

_____

_____

Guest Name

_____

_____

_____

_____

Guest Name

Wishes for the baby and
Tips for the parents

_____

_____

_____

_____

_____

Guest Name

Thoughts & Messages

_____

_____

_____

_____

_____

_____

Guest Name

_____

_____

_____

_____

_____

_____

Guest Name

Wishes for the baby and
Tips for the parents

_____

_____

_____

_____

_____

Guest Name

Thoughts & Messages

_____

_____

_____

_____

_____

Guest Name

_____

_____

_____

_____

Guest Name

Wishes for the baby and
Tips for the parents

_____

_____

_____

_____

_____

Guest Name

Thoughts & Messages

_____

_____

_____

_____

_____

Guest Name

_____

_____

_____

_____

Guest Name

Wishes for the baby and Tips for the parents

_____

_____

_____

_____

_____

Guest Name

Thoughts & Messages

_____

_____

_____

_____

_____

Guest Name

_____

_____

_____

_____

_____

Guest Name

Wishes for the baby and Tips for the parents

_____

_____

_____

_____

_____

Guest Name

Thoughts & Messages

_____

_____

_____

_____

_____

Guest Name

_____

_____

_____

_____

_____

Guest Name

Wishes for the baby and
Tips for the parents

_____

_____

_____

_____

Guest Name

Thoughts & Messages

_____

_____

_____

_____

_____

Guest Name

_____

_____

_____

_____

Guest Name

Wishes for the baby and Tips for the parents

_____

_____

_____

_____

_____

Guest Name

Thoughts & Messages

_____

_____

_____

_____

_____

Guest Name

_____

_____

_____

_____

_____

Guest Name

Wishes for the baby and
Tips for the parents

_____

_____

_____

_____

_____

Guest Name

Thoughts & Messages

Guest Name

Guest Name

Wishes for the baby and
Tips for the parents

_____

_____

_____

_____

_____

Guest Name

Thoughts & Messages

_____

_____

_____

_____

_____

Guest Name

_____

_____

_____

_____

_____

Guest Name

Wishes for the baby and Tips for the parents

_____

_____

_____

_____

_____

Guest Name

Thoughts & Messages

_____

_____

_____

_____

_____

Guest Name

_____

_____

_____

_____

Guest Name

Wishes for the baby and
Tips for the parents

_____

_____

_____

_____

_____

Guest Name

Thoughts & Messages

_____

_____

_____

_____

_____

_____

Guest Name

_____

_____

_____

_____

_____

Guest Name

Wishes for the baby and Tips for the parents

_____

_____

_____

_____

_____

Guest Name

Thoughts & Messages

_____

_____

_____

_____

_____

Guest Name

_____

_____

_____

_____

_____

Guest Name

Wishes for the baby and
Tips for the parents

_____

_____

_____

_____

Guest Name

Thoughts & Messages

_____

_____

_____

_____

_____

Guest Name

_____

_____

_____

_____

_____

Guest Name

Wishes for the baby and Tips for the parents

_____

_____

_____

_____

_____

Guest Name

Thoughts & Messages

Guest Name

Guest Name

Wishes for the baby and Tips for the parents

_____

_____

_____

_____

Guest Name

Thoughts & Messages

_____

_____

_____

_____

_____

Guest Name

_____

_____

_____

_____

_____

Guest Name

Wishes for the baby and
Tips for the parents

_____

_____

_____

_____

_____

Guest Name

Thoughts & Messages

_____

_____

_____

_____

_____

Guest Name

_____

_____

_____

_____

Guest Name

Wishes for the baby and Tips for the parents

_____

_____

_____

_____

_____

Guest Name

Thoughts & Messages

_____

_____

_____

_____

_____

Guest Name

_____

_____

_____

_____

Guest Name

Wishes for the baby and Tips for the parents

_____

_____

_____

_____

Guest Name

Thoughts & Messages

_____

_____

_____

_____

_____

Guest Name

_____

_____

_____

_____

Guest Name

Wishes for the baby and
Tips for the parents

_____

_____

_____

_____

Guest Name

Thoughts & Messages

_____

_____

_____

_____

_____

Guest Name

_____

_____

_____

_____

_____

Guest Name

Wishes for the baby and
Tips for the parents

_____

_____

_____

_____

_____

Guest Name

Thoughts & Messages

_____

_____

_____

_____

_____

Guest Name

_____

_____

_____

_____

Guest Name

Wishes for the baby and
Tips for the parents

_____

_____

_____

_____

Guest Name

Thoughts & Messages

_____

_____

_____

_____

_____

Guest Name

_____

_____

_____

_____

_____

Guest Name

Wishes for the baby and
Tips for the parents

_____

_____

_____

_____

_____

Guest Name

Thoughts & Messages

_____
_____
_____
_____
_____

Guest Name
_____
_____
_____
_____

Guest Name

Wishes for the baby and
Tips for the parents

_____

_____

_____

_____

_____

Guest Name

Thoughts & Messages

_____

_____

_____

_____

_____

Guest Name

_____

_____

_____

_____

_____

Guest Name

Wishes for the baby and
Tips for the parents

_____

_____

_____

_____

_____

Guest Name

Thoughts & Messages

Guest Name

Guest Name

Wishes for the baby and Tips for the parents

_____

_____

_____

_____

_____

Guest Name

Thoughts & Messages

_____

_____

_____

_____

_____

Guest Name

_____

_____

_____

_____

Guest Name

Wishes for the baby and
Tips for the parents

_____

_____

_____

_____

Guest Name

Thoughts & Messages

_____

_____

_____

_____

_____

Guest Name

_____

_____

_____

_____

Guest Name

Wishes for the baby and
Tips for the parents

_____

_____

_____

_____

_____

Guest Name

Thoughts & Messages

_____

_____

_____

_____

_____

Guest Name

_____

_____

_____

_____

_____

Guest Name

Wishes for the baby and
Tips for the parents

_____

_____

_____

_____

_____

Guest Name

Thoughts & Messages

_____

_____

_____

_____

_____

_____

Guest Name
_____

_____

_____

_____

_____

Guest Name

Wishes for the baby and
Tips for the parents

_____

_____

_____

_____

_____

Guest Name

Thoughts & Messages

_____

_____

_____

_____

_____

Guest Name

_____

_____

_____

_____

_____

Guest Name

Wishes for the baby and
Tips for the parents

_____

_____

_____

_____

_____

Guest Name

Thoughts & Messages

_____

_____

_____

_____

_____

Guest Name

_____

_____

_____

_____

Guest Name

Wishes for the baby and
Tips for the parents

_____

_____

_____

_____

_____

Guest Name

Thoughts & Messages

_____

_____

_____

_____

_____

Guest Name

_____

_____

_____

_____

Guest Name

Wishes for the baby and
Tips for the parents

_____

_____

_____

_____

_____

Guest Name

Thoughts & Messages

_____
_____
_____
_____
_____

Guest Name

_____
_____
_____
_____
_____

Guest Name

Wishes for the baby and
Tips for the parents

_____

_____

_____

_____

_____

Guest Name

Thoughts & Messages

_____
_____
_____
_____
_____

Guest Name
_____
_____
_____
_____

Guest Name

*Wishes for the baby and
Tips for the parents*

_____

_____

_____

_____

_____

Guest Name

Thoughts & Messages

_____

_____

_____

_____

_____

Guest Name

_____

_____

_____

_____

_____

Guest Name

Wishes for the baby and Tips for the parents

_____

_____

_____

_____

_____

Guest Name

Thoughts & Messages

_____

_____

_____

_____

_____

Guest Name
_____

_____

_____

_____

_____

Guest Name

Wishes for the baby and
Tips for the parents

_____

_____

_____

_____

Guest Name

Thoughts & Messages

Guest Name

Guest Name

Wishes for the baby and
Tips for the parents

_____

_____

_____

_____

_____

Guest Name

Thoughts & Messages

_____
_____
_____
_____

Guest Name

_____
_____
_____
_____

Guest Name

Wishes for the baby and Tips for the parents

_____

_____

_____

_____

_____

Guest Name

Thoughts & Messages

_____

_____

_____

_____

_____

Guest Name

_____

_____

_____

_____

Guest Name

Wishes for the baby and
Tips for the parents

_____

_____

_____

_____

_____

Guest Name

Thoughts & Messages

_____

_____

_____

_____

_____

Guest Name

_____

_____

_____

_____

_____

Guest Name

Wishes for the baby and
Tips for the parents

_____

_____

_____

_____

_____

Guest Name

Thoughts & Messages

_____
_____
_____
_____
_____

Guest Name

_____
_____
_____
_____
_____

Guest Name

Wishes for the baby and
Tips for the parents

_____

_____

_____

_____

_____

Guest Name

Thoughts & Messages

_____

_____

_____

_____

_____

_____

Guest Name

_____

_____

_____

_____

_____

Guest Name

Wishes for the baby and
Tips for the parents

_____

_____

_____

_____

_____

Guest Name

Thoughts & Messages

_____

_____

_____

_____

_____

Guest Name
_____

_____

_____

_____

Guest Name

Wishes for the baby and Tips for the parents

_____

_____

_____

_____

_____

Guest Name

Thoughts & Messages

_____

_____

_____

_____

_____

Guest Name

_____

_____

_____

_____

_____

Guest Name

Wishes for the baby and
Tips for the parents

_____

_____

_____

_____

Guest Name

Thoughts & Messages

_____

_____

_____

_____

_____

Guest Name

_____

_____

_____

_____

_____

Guest Name

Wishes for the baby and
Tips for the parents

_____

_____

_____

_____

_____

Guest Name

Thoughts & Messages

_____

_____

_____

_____

_____

Guest Name

_____

_____

_____

_____

Guest Name

Wishes for the baby and
Tips for the parents

_____

_____

_____

_____

_____

Guest Name

Thoughts & Messages

_____

_____

_____

_____

_____

Guest Name

_____

_____

_____

_____

_____

Guest Name

Wishes for the baby and
Tips for the parents

_____

_____

_____

_____

_____

Guest Name

Thoughts & Messages

_____

_____

_____

_____

_____

Guest Name

_____

_____

_____

_____

Guest Name

Made in the USA
Las Vegas, NV
14 January 2024

84379575R00057